101 Super Uses
for Tampon Applicators

by Lori Katz and Barb Meyer

♡ Dedicated to the Special Women in our lives who introduced us to the World of feminine hygiene.

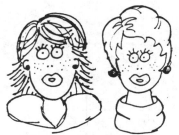

Georgeann & Iris

High Stress Press™

Library of Congress Catalog Card Number
94-78293

10 9 8 7 6 5 4 3

Katz, Lori; Meyer, Barb.
101 Super Uses for Tampon Applicators: a helpful guide for
the environmentally conscious consumer of feminine
hygiene products / written and illustrated
by Lori Katz and Barb Meyer

ISBN 0-9641907-0-2

Published in the U.S.A. by

High Stress Press™
ŏŏ ŏŏ

531 Main Street Suite 668
El Segundo, CA 90245-0037

THIRD EDITION

Trade Orders:

Book Trade: LPC Group 1-800-626-4330
Gift Trade: Sourcebooks 1-800-727-8866

tampon applicator \ˈtəm-pänˈap-lə-ˌkāt-ər\

noun. mechanical device (plastic or cardboard) used for inserting tampons in order to prevent embarassing situations.

- imagine the number of women each year who use tampons.

- think about how many tampons are used each year! gross thought.

- it is rumored that 700 tampon applicators were found on the shores of New Jersey during the late 1980's.

- lori found one by her car in Santa Monica yesterday morning on her way to work.

- Scientists believe in the year 2000, there will be more tampon applicators than people

- tampon applicators will outlive your dog, your cat, ... perhaps all of mankind.

- and besides tampon applicators are too good to throw away.

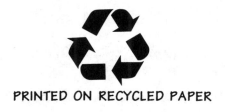

PRINTED ON RECYCLED PAPER

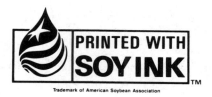

We paid extra for these.
(aren't we great!)

Chapters

1. Fashion Accessories
2. Beauty Secrets
3. Travel Tips
4. Toys and School Projects
5. Car Detailing
6. Entertaining
7. Lifestyles
8. Holidays and Special Occasions
9. Good House Keeping
10. Babies and Pets
11. Crafts and Home Decor
12. Emergency Uses
13. Miscellaneous

1

Fashion Accessories

Queen for a day Jewelry
+ just cut and create and decorate with RHINESTONES!
tiara: glue applicators on old visor
earrings: cut and slide on!
Necklace & Bracelet → just cut and string 'em together!
you can even make nails.

FASHION
EYEGLASS
ROLLBAR
Decorate with rhinestones!

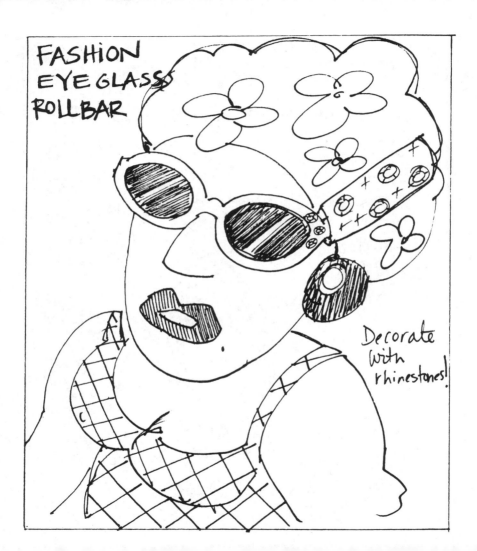

Zipper Pulls for the Whole family.
.decorate for holiday themes too!
—comb over hairstyle.
members only

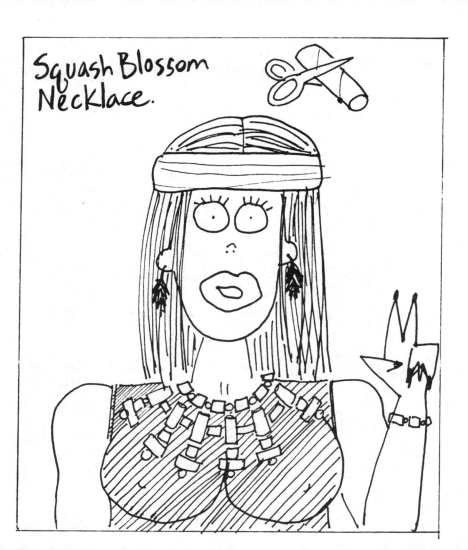

Squash Blossom
Necklace.

Crochet High Fashion Garments
cut tampon applicator lengthwise (just one cut)
cut desired holes down sides
crochet your favorite stitch and decorate

Bolo tie (and matching HAT decoration)

*·you know the trick...: decorate with rhinestones etc.

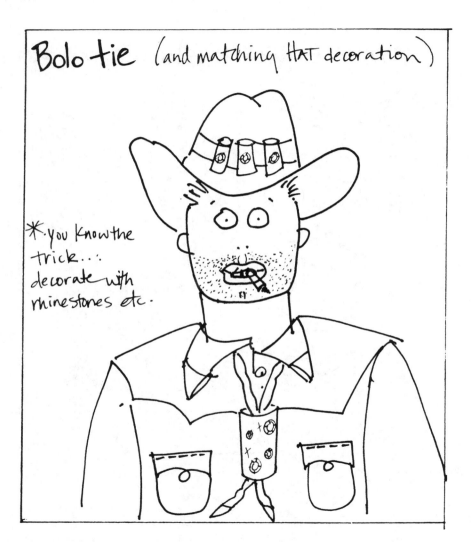

Bitchin' Beach Sandals
·Find tampon applicators on the beach.
·Stick one inside another.
·string together with old fishing line
add elastic band from old underwear.
·Maybe use a tire tread for sole.
STUSSY

Decorative Cover for Pens

· add rhinestones, feathers and silk flowers to applicator, slip over pen!

Dear Marge
I can't believe
She told me
Betty

Worry Doll Pin (for when you dont get your period)
OH Shit....
• Dip tip of applicator in glue and roll in gravel (Hair)
• Wrap with burlap cloth
• Wrap yarn around middle for top
• Draw the face
• Glue to Pin

Hair Plaits
10

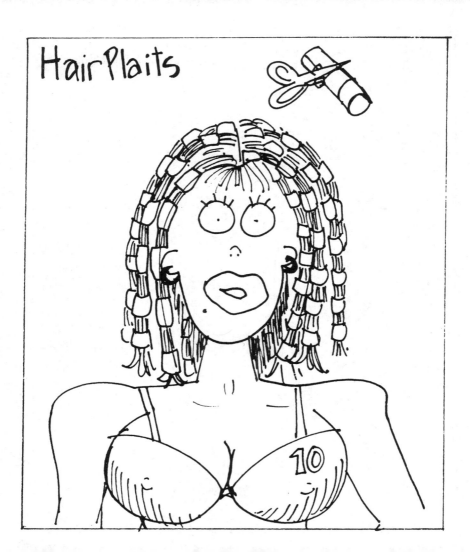

Cool Person Cigarette Holder
(Rug... shsh)
ART
OPENING
cocktail franks
included

African Necklace
cut and string together to fit neck.

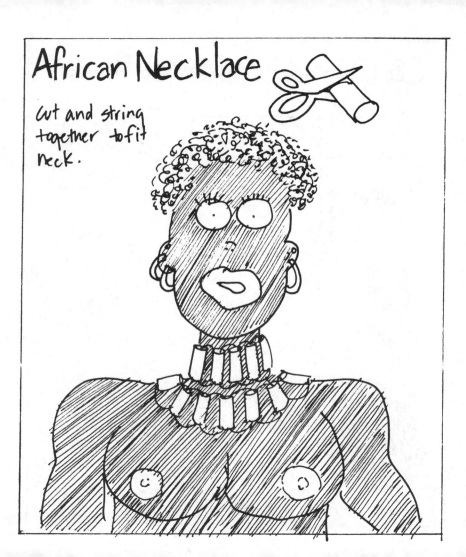

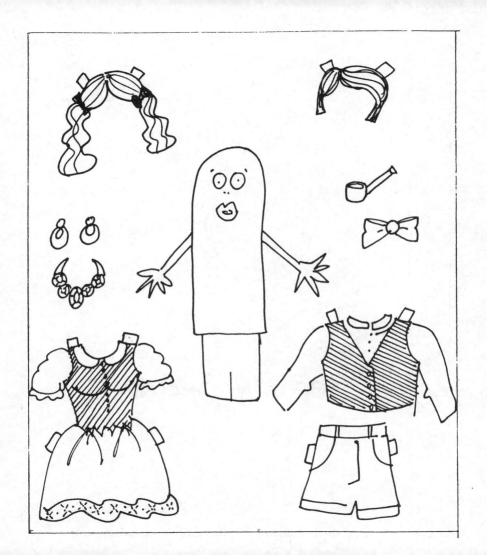

2

Beauty Secrets

Wrist and Ankle Weights
for
(Sweatin' to the Oldies!)
•Collect 6 applicators for each ankle and 4 for each wrist.
•Fill with sand
•Hot glue to terry cloth sweatbands and slip on.
ROCK out!

No More Callous Handle

CALLOUS B·GONE!

- cut applicator straight across.

- Snap over ordinary handles on bags

Rodeo Drive

- use both inside and outside applicator for extra strength
- If you want, take home and decorate

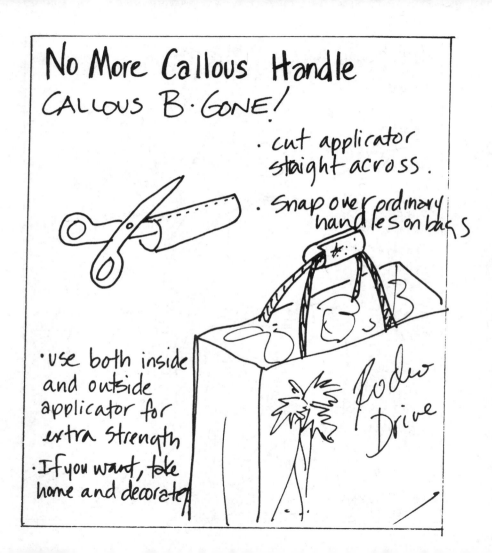

hair Curlers
① first, cut open outer tube
②
③
Wind hair around inside tube
Snap outer tube over hair
leave in over-night for glamourous curls.
SAVE MONEY! $@$ ☺

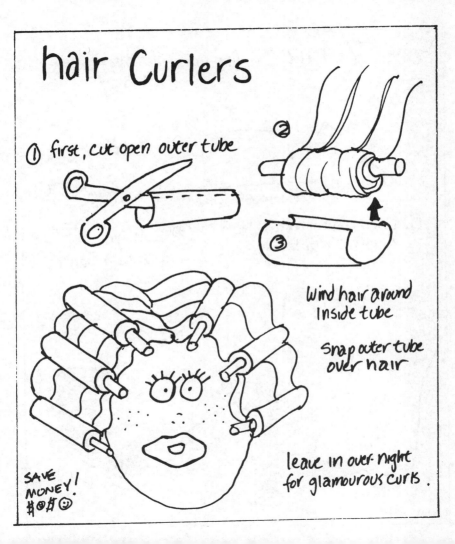

Foot Pumice (No one likes to suck a callous!)

double stick tape

① wind double stick tape around applicator

② Roll in gravel + sand

Secretary Wrist guard.
· Bunch & wrap 6 applicators with a rubberband.
· stick hand thru.
· slide up to wrist.
Could Help to prevent carpal tunnel Syndrome

For Flawless toenails

Gently
- place applicators between toes
- Have a Tab w/ a slice of lemon
- paint nails

hot red &

- Watch Oprah and wait 20 minutes.

Personalized Perfume Necklace
spray your favorite perfume on a sponge
stuff in applicator
punch in some holes and string
ooo..
i think its working!
WOW

Travel Tips

tooth Brush Protector

- Never let your toothbrush fall prey to the Nasties in your makeup Bag

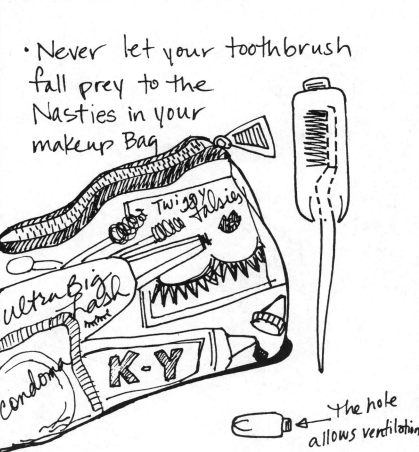

the hole allows ventilation

Travel Sewing Kit
throw in a couple of buttons
wrap your favorite color thread around applicator, hold at top of applicator in slots
Just throw it in your makeup bag and GO!
makeup

Travel Abacus
死鬼佬
真混帳!
What can I get for this much?

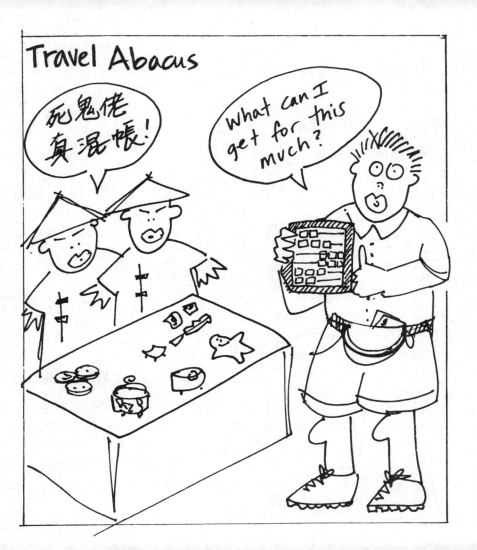

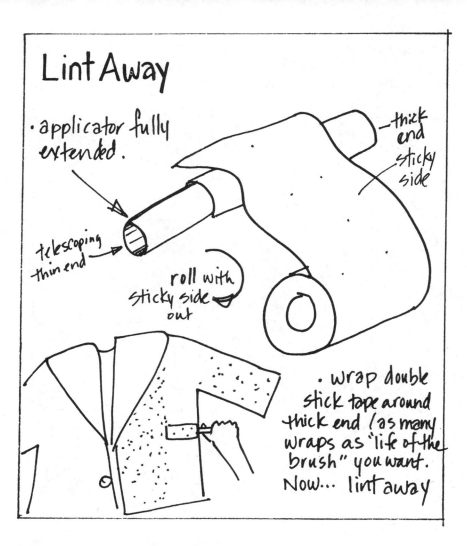

Lint Away

• applicator fully extended.

telescoping thin end

thick end sticky side

roll with sticky side out

• wrap double stick tape around thick end (as many wraps as "life of the brush" you want. Now... lint away your ideas here....

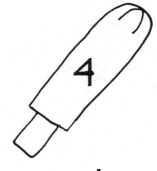

Toys and
School Projects

TOY BANDALERO
lookout Rambo!
MAKE MY DAY

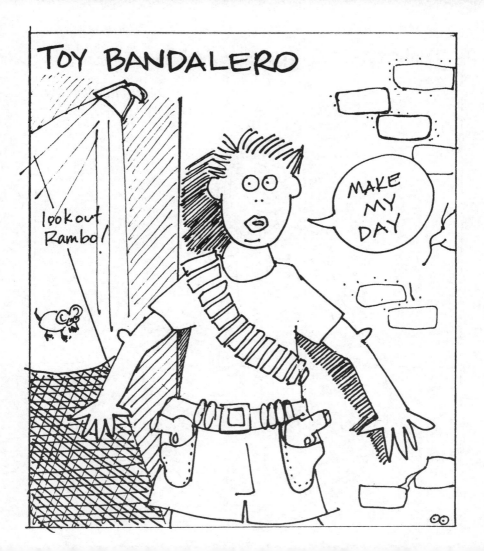

INSTANT JumpRope
just string together
and knot!

Finger Puppets

supplies:
pipe cleaners
applicators
yarn
eyeballs
old doll clothes
old ring
cigarband

this one is Romeo
fingergoeshere

Romeo & Juliette
OH Romeo!

- We think you can figure this out.
- If not....
  the old ring becomes a crown and the cigar band is a hat for Romeo.

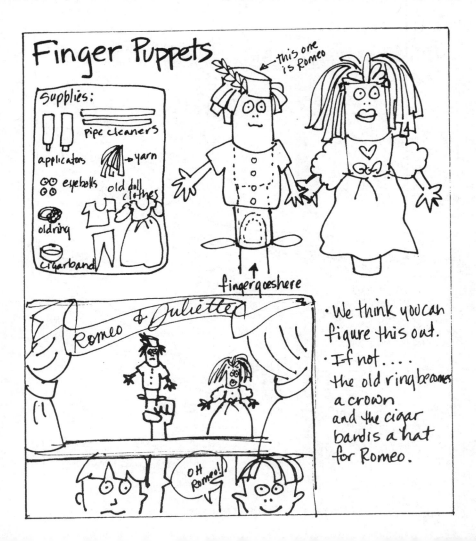

James Bond Snorkle
TIFFANY... Where are YOU? It's time to clean your room!
6 Ft.
DEEP
* First try in really shallow water

Lint Toy Animals

- **Supplies:**
  - eyeballs
  - mini pompom ball
  - pipe cleaners
  - tampon applicator
  - double stick
  - paper cone
  - tongue & ears out of construction paper
  - dryer lint
  - glue

- roll applicator in doublestick
- then roll applicator w/ double stick in dryer lint.
- twist pipe cleaners like this
- (these become legs & tail!)
- use a pen as a guide
- Glue paper cone on one end and tail on other.
- Plug on legs
- Glue on details (eyes, nose, ears)

Child's Inexpensive Billiard Set!
never play for $$ (too many variables)
*Create your pool stick by telescoping applicators ontop of one another.
*use whiffle balls or ping pong balls
Start having fun!

Starship Enterprise Model Kit
Would someone plleeasse Beam me up!!!
NCC1701
USS ENTERPRISE
Kleen X
.Stack paper plates together.
.Glue together tissue box and applicators like above
.Push orange & red tissue paper in applicator ends for flames.
.Use a Red and Black marker for details
make Spock ears

Tampon Dolls from Around the World
I'd like to teach the World to sing...
...in perfect harmony...

TOY Binoculars

- cut holes in paper plate for eye location, nose for smooth fit and mouth for breathing

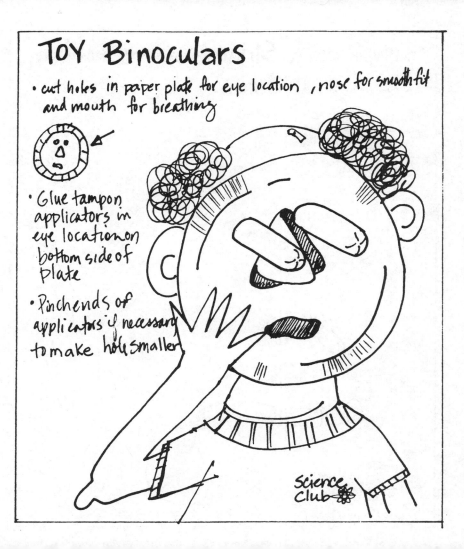

- Glue tampon applicators in eye location on bottom side of plate

- Pinch ends of applicators if necessary to make hole smaller

Science Club

Snake on a String – just string 'em along

- ADD EYES and rattler
- Play tricks on friends

Spit Wad Shooter
SPLAT!
OH MY!
BIBL
HIGH TIMES

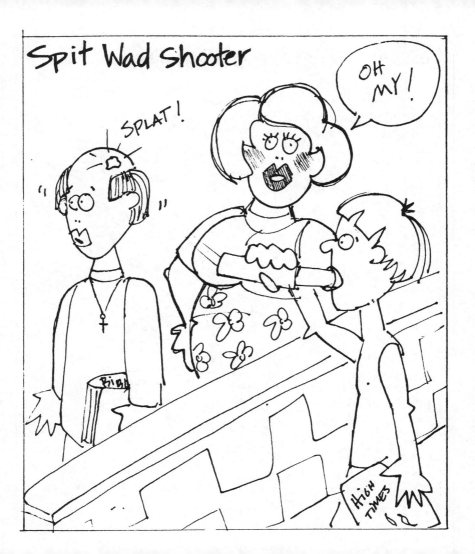

Growing Potatoe Head Dolls

LOG CABIN
construction paper roof
Cut door in old shoe box.
Glue
squeeze tube paint for decorating
Pin becomes door knob!
• Glue applicators to shoe box for log cabin look.
• Paint if you like!
The Texas
We come in Peace.... Take these gifts!
Find out how to make figures on page 17.

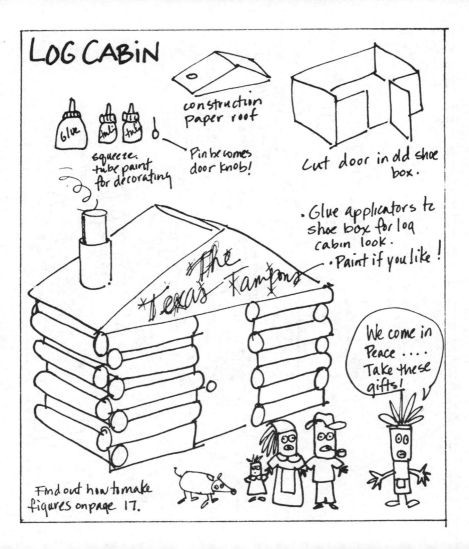

Foozball Replacement Player

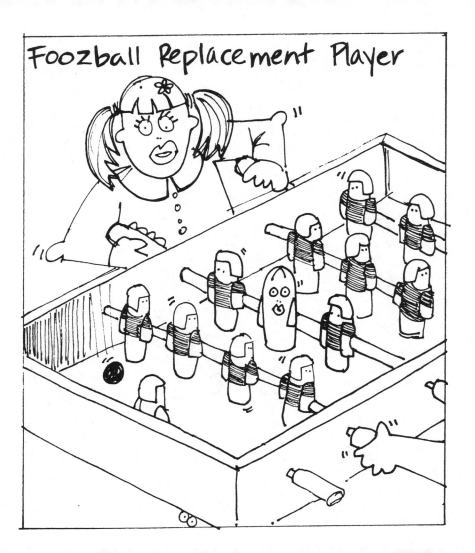

Halloween Costumes Galore!
Bucky Beaver or Bunny
You know who this is!
FK
extend finger tips to length you want!
The Vamp

Doll Raft (for the tub or pool!)
string together as many rows as you need!
Works best with 11½" dolls.

Chinese Finger Trap
... what is one anyway ???

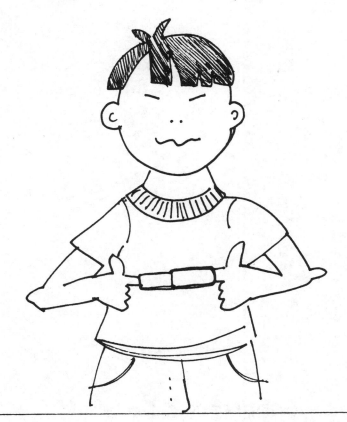

Connect the Dots

5

Car Detailing

Car Seat Covers
(the beaded look)
• Keep the small part of applicator inside the large part.
• Shellac for hardness
Never sit on crumbs again, they all fall through
this one takes Patience

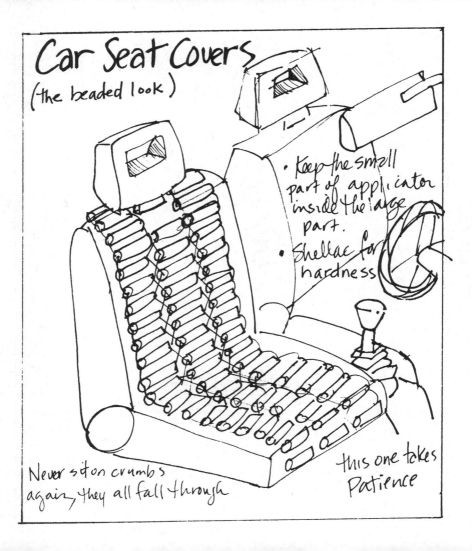

Pine tree air freshener

fill center applicator with pot pourri
cut in sections
cut again and slide over center
ticket
Ford

6

Entertaining

Fireplace Starter
Gas
coffee can
roll old newspapers really tight
• plug into tampon applicator
• add a couple drops of lighter fluid
• store in old coffee can for quick romantic evenings
extras
"you really know how to light my fire..."

Hors d'oeuvre Serving Assistant
I'm having a Martha Stewart Day!
Would you like one?
Marge, I love your Moo Moo

Mini Chinese Lanterns
use Christmas lights (the tiny ones)
cut slits in tampon (be careful)
*Turn your Backyard into a party palace.
chef

Cool Freezer Pops
cool & tasty snacks for hot summer days!
cool & whip
·plug ends (with gum)
·Fit applicators tightly in container (coolwhip)
·Fill with juice
And Freeze!
cool pops

Party Favors
M&MS
tie with ribbon
2521
Jan, thanks so much... you're so sweet.. here's a little something
Baby Sho

Your favorite Creation

Paste
Polaroid
Here

7

Lifestyles

FINGER EXTENDERS
for hours of
piano playing.

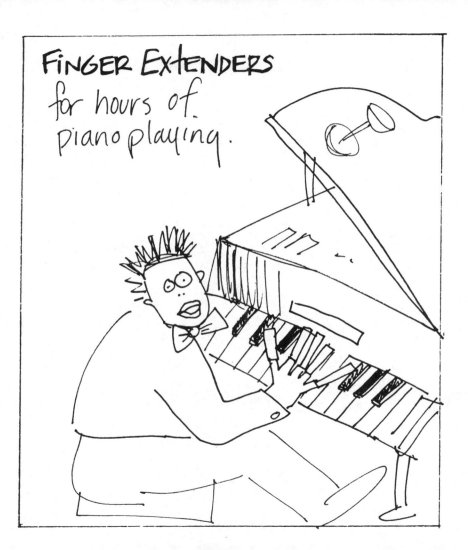

Hanky Holder for BIG RALLYS
(this is all you need to start!)
with a pencil push through cut end (pretty deep) then pull back out just enough to be full.
Use for:
· Homecoming Parades
· Political Speeches
· Concerts
Fight.
Freedom
less filling
Yeah
metoo.

Spoke Decorator

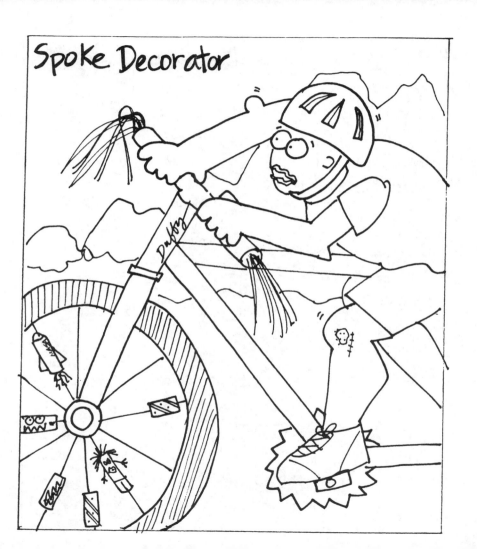

Pool Lane Dividers
Keep Moving!
DEEP
Fred

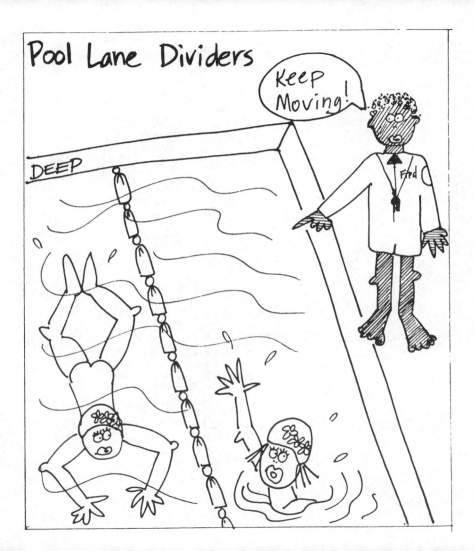

Water Bottle Caddy
for Power Walking

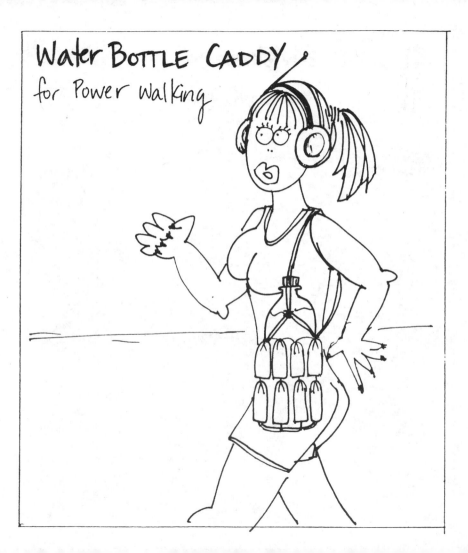

Fishing Bobber
beer
thats the nicest bobber I've seen all day

Hammock

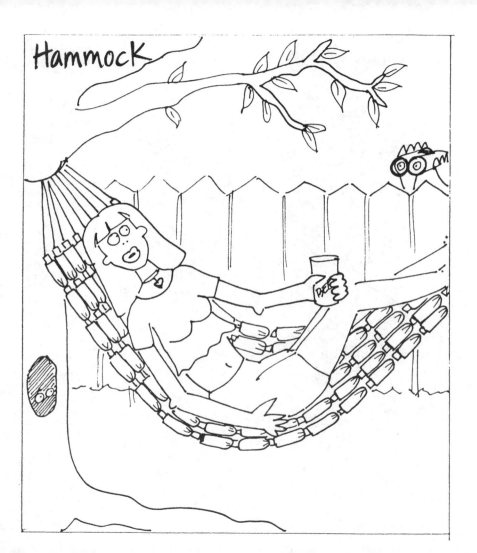

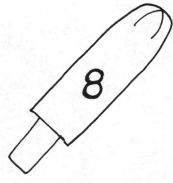

8

Holidays & Special
Occasions

Hanukkah Menorah
• Hot glue an applicator to a paper plate (glue that to the mantle.
• Glue nine additional applicators on top... Add candles + decorate!
Baruch ata adenoi...

Xmas tree Ornaments
NOEL
Earl
Patsy

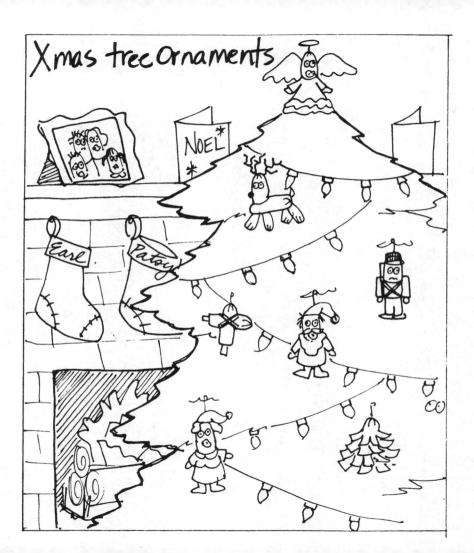

Confetti Shooter
Surprise!
R. Feldman
CEO
MS

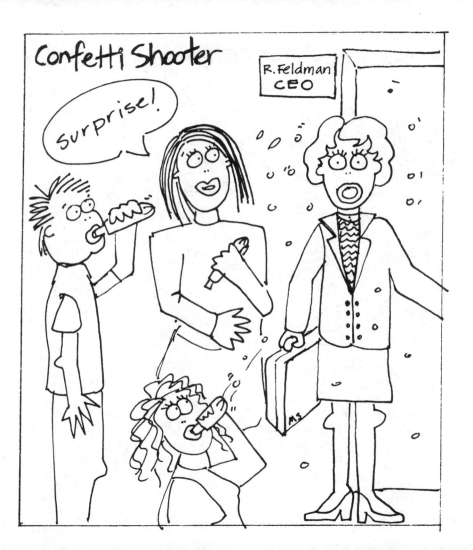

Nativity Scene (christmas trees & Jesus)

cut about halfway up in 1/8" to 1/4" strips

→ tree

lint

stack 'em & paint green

& add drier lint for texture.

* Refer to page for making Jesus + friends

Icing Squirter
Happy Birthday
Betty
Fill applicator with your FAV icing.
· Use inside applicator to push icing out
· Make rosettes

Holiday Wreath
Who's there?... ... Noel? ....
MAIL
D
·cut out cardboard donut
·Hot glue applicators to donut
·Sprinkle with glitter rhinestones + berries!
ADD A BOW!

tooth fairy tooth holder
Hi tooth fairy give me more $
toothfairy can easily eject tooth or teeth
-include special messages to the tooth fairy on little pieces of paper
* put under pillow T.F. will know what it is!

scratch
-n- sniff

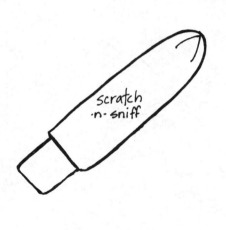

Good Housekeeping

EMERGENCY CLOTHES PINS
cut halfway up
HINT
*Use smaller part for tighter grip
slide cut end over clothes and Voilà!
REO Speedwagon

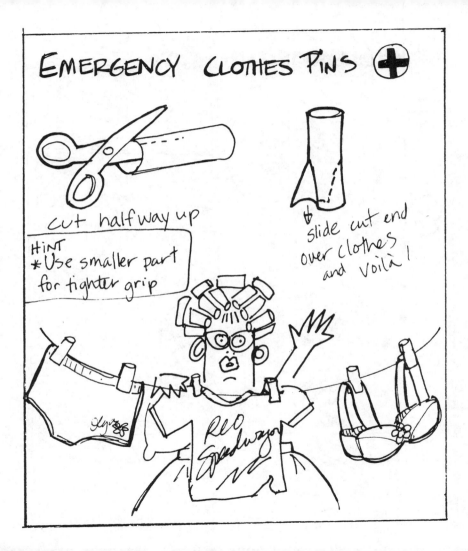

Olive Grabber
Fridge
olive oil
olive bread
tampons

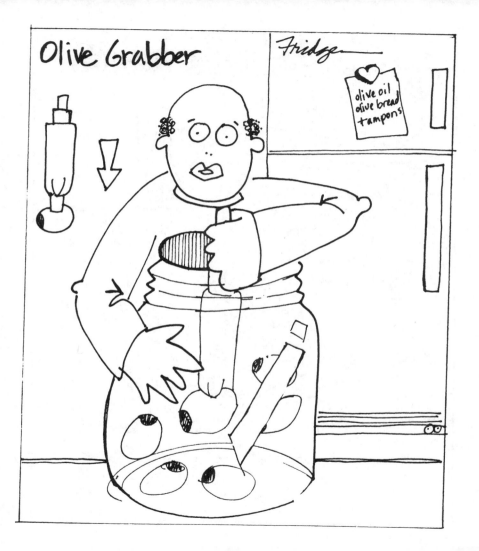

Litter Box Poo Remover (its easy)
Flushable applicators makes it a snap (it just makes sense)
I ♥ CATS
Kitty's Throne
Keep a few handy in an old cool whip container
cool whip

Drawer Sachet
place potpourri in a fancy lace handkerchief
stuff into applicator tube
Place in underwear drawer or any place thats "not so fresh".

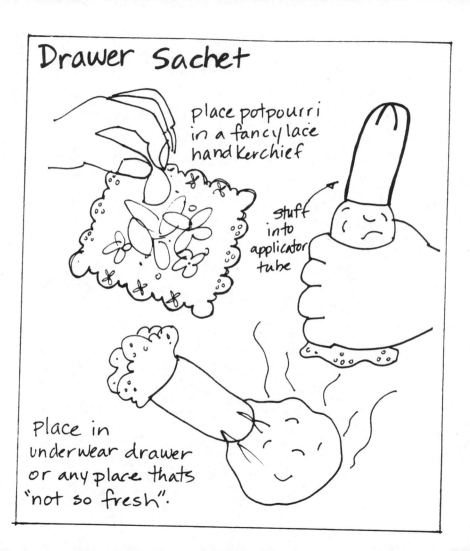

Gardener's Little Helper Seed Planter
• stick seed in applicator
• push tip in ground & push out.
seeds

Birdfeeder
(in one minute!)
roll in honey
seeds
Try other treats like granola/peanut butter popcorn... Also check with a pet store to see if these food items are even o.k!

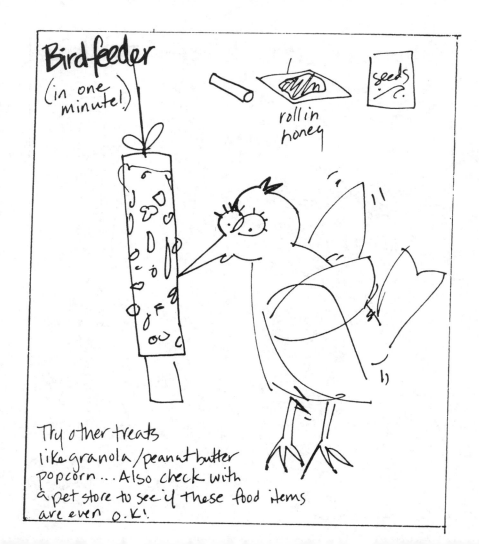

Spaghetti Measurer
spaghettioroni
• fill outer tube of applicator with raw spaghetti
♥ measuring the right amount of spaghetti is no longer a problem!
• just empty contents into boiling water
easy handle for breaking spaghetti in half.

Drip Irrigation

cut old Kitchen sponges into strips.
find a regular no. 2 pencil
stuff sponge strip into tampon applicator
rubberband applicator onto pencil ... soak with water

Babies and Pets

Doggie Tail & Ear Splints
·Have your doggie ears lost their umph?
·Has Spot been pushed around the neighborhood one time too many?
No More....
Now the coolest dog on the block!
BONE

Kitty Brush
for hours of bonding with your favorite feline!
cover applicator with double stick tape
• replace when full of Fur!
LazyBoy

Hamster Treadmill
make two pieces like this ↓
Assemble
ADD SCENERY
Glacier water
Dont BANG ON GLASS!

Baby Teether
① string together
(limit number of applicatois, so ring cannot fit over babies head!)
② Stick in freezer for 1 hour, and serve!

Doggie I.D. tag

"scraps" I belong to Goober Pyle..
Oohh scraps... Here boy!
fifi
scraps
· write name and address on piece of paper
· roll up + stick in applicator
· attach to dog collar

Cat Toy (made with love)
CAT NIP
fill tampon applicator with Kitty's favorite catnip!
• tie a string around end and make a pretty bowl.
• you can decorate with puffy paint
fluffy
• or make it look like a mouse!
they make great gifts too!

Your personal logbook of tampon applicators

MONTH	PLASTIC	PAPER	DAY 1	PLASTIC	PAPER	DAY 2	PLASTIC	PAPER	DAY 3	PLASTIC	PAPER	DAY 4	PLASTIC	PAPER	DAY 5
JAN															
FEB															
MAR															
APRIL															
MAY															
JUNE															
JULY															
AUG.															
SEPT.															
OCT.															
NOV.															
DEC.															
TOTALS:															

11

Crafts & Home Decor

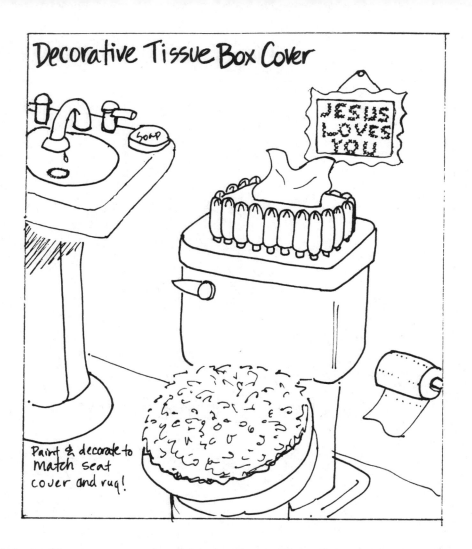

Decorative Tissue Box Cover

JESUS LOVES YOU

Paint & decorate to match seat cover and rug!

Decorative Flowers

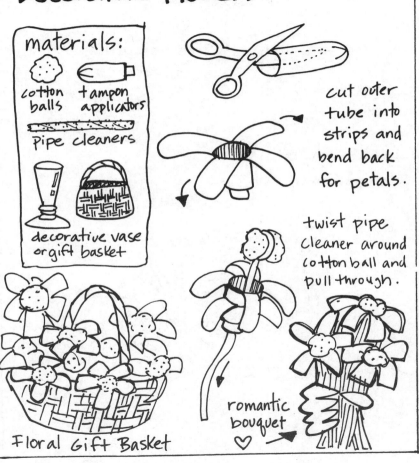

materials:

cotton balls

tampon applicators

pipe cleaners

decorative vase or gift basket

cut outer tube into strips and bend back for petals.

twist pipe cleaner around cotton ball and pull through.

Floral Gift Basket

romantic bouquet ♡

RING HOLDER

1. Find a chunk of styrofoam ... the kind florist use

2. Push applicators in foam so they are sturdy. Some glue may be required.

3. Decorate with wire flowers and rhinestones

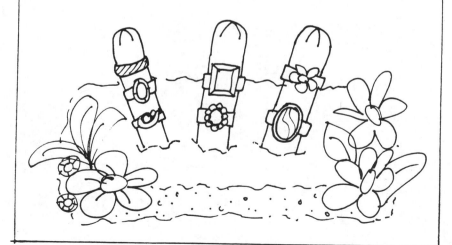

CD RACK
1• Poke holes into styrofoam with a sharp pencil.
Paint to match IKEA decor
(BLACK is cool!!)
2• Glue applicators in holes

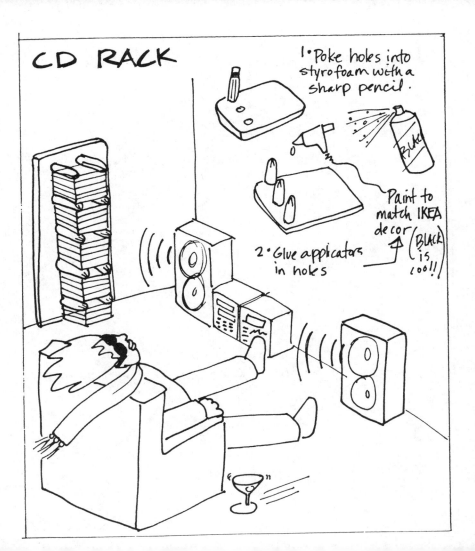

Napkin Rings

- cut length wise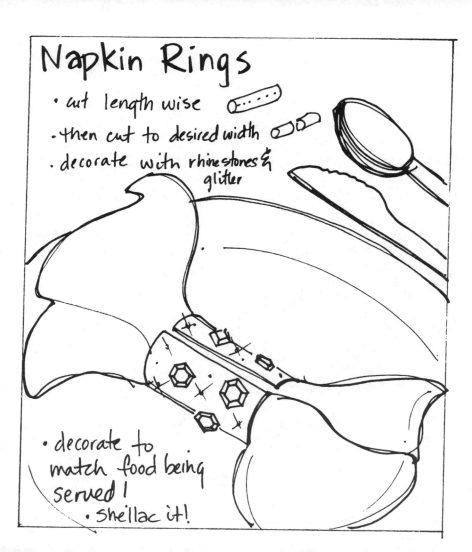
- then cut to desired width
- decorate with rhinestones & glitter

- decorate to match food being served!
  - shellac it!

Groovy Doorway Beads
Purple

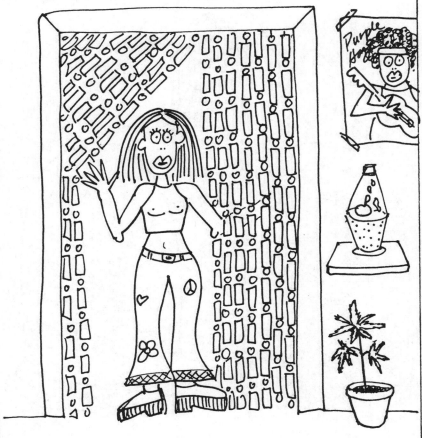

Celebrity Collector Dolls!
cher
Elvis♡
Marilyn

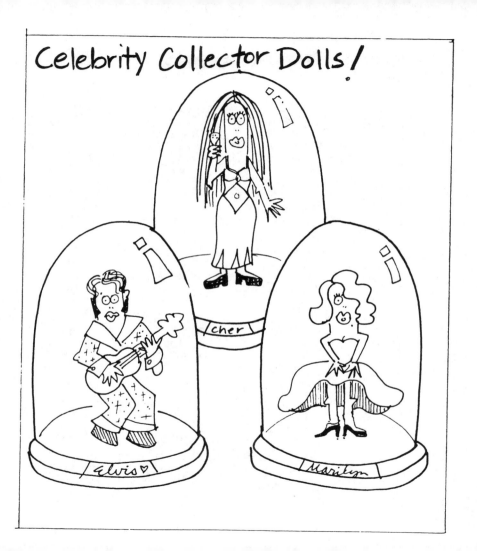

Beautiful Picture Frames
① cut once
② Decorate
③ Slide on!
P.S. Don't forget about the rhinestones

Emergency Uses

Pain Grip
· also use when taking out splinters
· burning off ticks
· applying alcohol to cuts
· tweezing eyebrows
· using any epilady product
· removing arrows

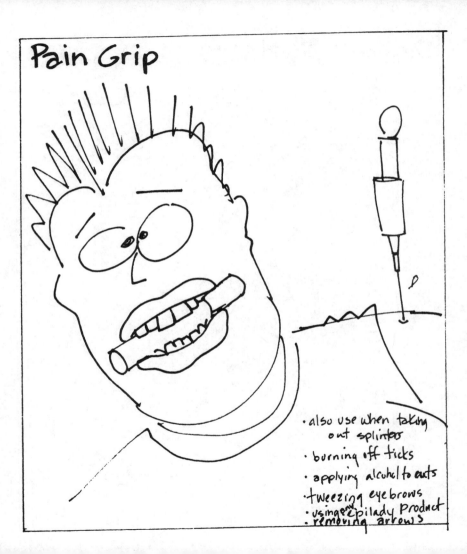

Distress Messages
HELP

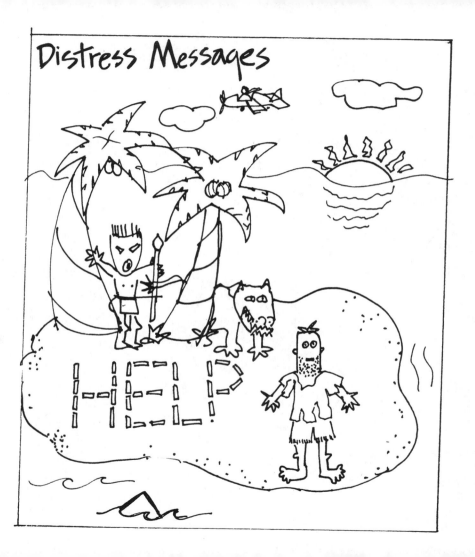

Hide a Key
(who would want to look)
WELCOME

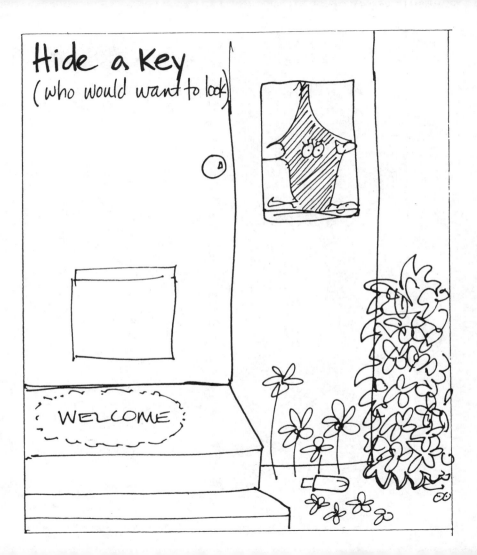

Backyard Wildlife First Aid Splints
leave some extra by the garbage.
Stay away from my pellets ... I'm warning you!

Emergency Stoma
·air flows easily through wide opening.
magnified view
·Only trained professionals should try this!

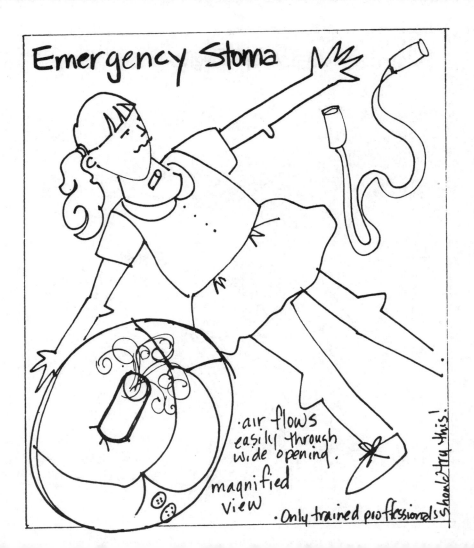

Whiplash Neck Brace
BEEEEEEEEP
Hint:
Always wear a seatbelt!
· You can decorate to coordinate with wardrobe!

Emergency Secret Mint Dispenser
1 load certs or tictacs
2: Replace small part of applicator and use to dispense!
rhinestone personalization
you'll see even the coolest using them

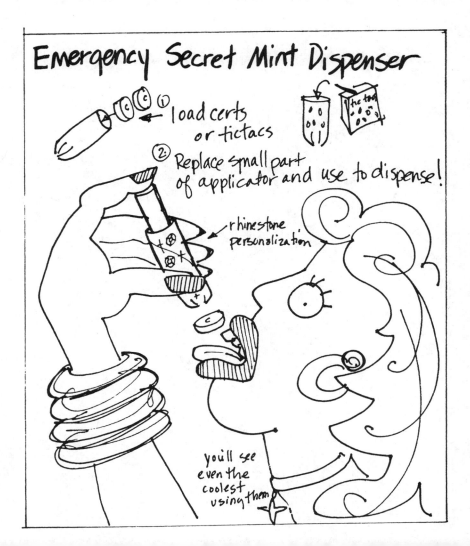

Emergency Wedding Bands
The ring!?
I forgot the ring!!!
I've got something Here!
His
Hers
or
Now glue on a jewel!

Miscellaneous

PUBLIC ART
for hours of viewing...
even the weather conditions
won't break it down!
oh my!
"Phallus"
For the people
of
Cincinnati
LGC

MONEY HIDE AWAY
roll up $ into applicator
reassemble, hide in box
TAMPONS
TAMPONS
Ssshhh!

Handy Voodoo Doll
Pat.... Did you do what I asked you to do!
Far Side
Patricia Bradley
94 Day Runner
★ all you need is a marker, photo of person and a couple of Pins!

Backyard Sundial
just clear a spot!

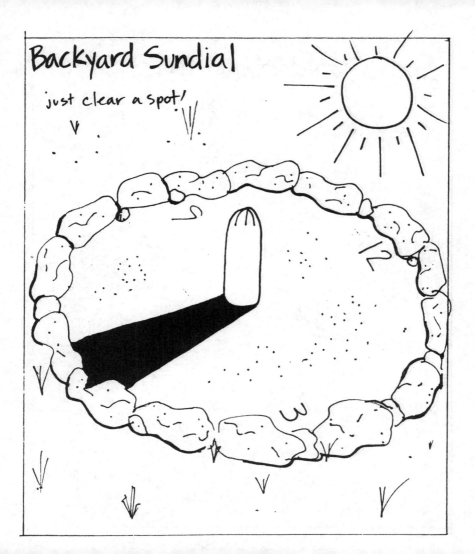

Ice Skating Blade Protector
(No more dulling blades)
slide 'em on!
Just Do It.... I love soup...
NK

RABBIT FOOT LUCKY charm.

Things you need:

tampon
applicator

dryer
lint

toenails
(dogs, birds, chicken)
grandpas

① Double stick
tape wrapped
around tampon.

② Roll tampon
in dryer lint

③ Glue on toenails
for the
"real feel"

OO
Add eyes if you
think its necessary

Zen Garden

Cotton Candy Sticks
Buckeye Snacks
OHIO
ALVIN
Ohio
state
Fair

Classroom Pointer
FATHER CROSS
REDUCE
RECYCLE
REUSE
I will not litter
I will not litter
I will not li

TAMPON
world
LEGO
land
The Worlds Favorite
11½" Applicator
Tammy Tampon
& Scraps
AiSLE 2
DOlls
HOT
NEW
Item
Soldier Man

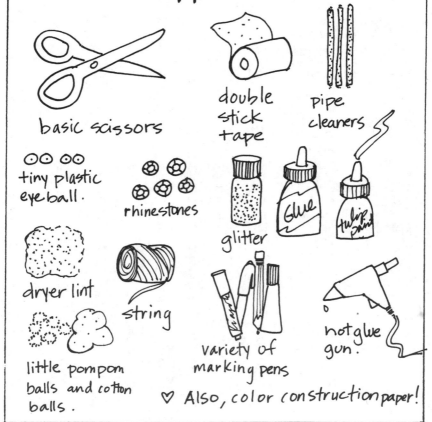

Some of our favorite Craft tools and supplies

basic scissors

double stick tape

pipe cleaners

tiny plastic eye ball.

rhinestones

glitter

Glue

tulip paint

dryer lint

string

variety of marking pens

hot glue gun.

little pompom balls and cotton balls.

♡ Also, color construction paper!

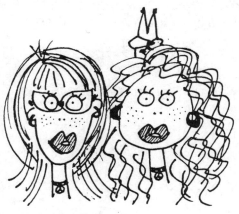

TWO
white girls from the
Midwest ™

TO ORDER MORE COPIES

SEND YOUR CHECK OR MONEY ORDER FOR $12.00
(includes shipping and handling) PAYABLE TO:

High Stress Press™

P.O. Box 37   El Segundo, CA   90245

- -

Please Print: Your Name _____

Address _____

State _____   Zip Code _____

Save on Multiple Orders!

Number of copies ordered

_____

Total enclosed

$ _____

Order 2 or more copies to the same address for only $10 each!